The Deadly Streets of Yorkshire

Gerald Burns

Copyright © 2021 – Gerald Burns

All rights reserved.

No part of this publication may be reproduced, stored in a retrieval system, or transmitted, in any form or by any means, electronic, mechanical, photocopying, recording or otherwise, without the prior written permission of the author.

Introduction
Peter Sutcliffe's Early Life
Marriage to Sonia
A cheating mother
Peter's First attempted murder
The first recorded case
The Real Reign of Terror begins
Wilma McCann
Emily Jackson
Irene Richardson
Patricia Atkinson
Jane McDonald
Jean Jordan
The detectives are careless once again
The Ripper Strikes again
Barbara Leach
Marguerite Walls
Mo Lea's lucky escape and survival
Jacqueline Hills
The Yorkshire Ripper is caught
Peter Sutcliffe's Trial

Battle with mental health and death

References

Other Books by Gerald Burns

About The Author

Introduction

On the 2nd of January, 1981, Britain breathed a sigh a relief when a killer who had taken the life of over 13 women was apprehended at Melbourne Avenue by two policemen. The killer had escaped identification and arrest for over five years, and his capture was a relief for the women of Yorkshire.

His name was Peter Sutcliffe and the press were calling him 'The Yorkshire Ripper", whose brutal modus operandi involved attacking helpless ladies with a hammer before stabbing them to death with a screwdriver and dismembering their body.

During his reign of terror, the streets of Yorkshire became quieter with the stories of murdered women who had fallen prey to this serial killer. In the dark lurked this psychopathic figure called 'The Yorkshire Ripper". Britons quaked at the mention of this serial killer who terrified the nation with his hammer and screwdriver. This smart psychopath seemed to derive a lot of pleasure from watching women die painful deaths. He seemed to enjoy every moment of their torture.

Described as a ruthless and cold-hearted killer, investigators confirmed that the murderer enjoyed going out at night and killing just for the thrill of it. And by the time he was captured by the police, Peter Sutcliffe had arguably become one of Britain's most prolific serial killer. His apprehension brought an end to a manhunt that literally shook Britain and some neighboring countries.

For the period he remained elusive, Sutcliffe was a thorn in the flesh of detectives at West Yorkshire Police. They never knew when he would attack next and his moves were largely unpredictable. The Northern part of England was soaked in the horror and gloomy stories of the killer at night – The Yorkshire Ripper.

Here is the story of Peter Sutcliffe.

Peter Sutcliffe's Early Life

Peter Sutcliffe was born on the 2nd of June, 1946 in the small town of Bingley just outside of Bradford, West Yorkshire. He was the last amongst many elder siblings who were very much older than him and worked to earn a living for themselves and support the family. Because of this, Peter spent most of his growing up days alone with his mother in their Bradford home.

Peter was a shy boy who adored his mother, Kathleen Frances. Kathleen suffered a lot of control and domination from her husband, John Sutcliffe, and Peter developed some sympathy for her. Peter thought the world of his mother and did all he could to support her as a child.

The events of his earlier days would go on to shape much of Peter's later life, evident in his weird career choices.

Peter Sutcliffe had a variety of jobs as an adult. He worked as a gravedigger for a while, with reports of him stealing things from the bodies after they'd been buried. He was never repulsed by the thought of searching through a dead person's casket to find valuables. That was a first sign of the problems to come in his future.

Marriage to Sonia

When he was 21, Peter met Sonia Sherman on Valentine's day of 1967. They had a long relationship which culminated into their marriage about seven years later, in August 1974. Their marriage was an admirable one, without any issues of sexual or domestic violence recorded. It is believed that Peter adored the women around him who he considered to be useful as his nurturers and care givers. He looked at Sonia the same way he looked at his mother, with the same adoration and love.

In Peter's eyes, he saw women as two things: The ones close to him were perfect angels to be protected and adored while anyone outside of his close circle were basically objects to be used for his gratification. His opposing ideas about women shattered after he discovered his mother had been cheating on his father.

A cheating mother

When the revelation of Kathleen's extramarital affair came to light, the 23-year-old Peter experienced a mental breakdown. Someone he looked to all his life had failed him through her unfaithfulness. Kathleen was seeing a policeman and Peter felt it wise to report the issue to his father. The two of them went to confront her in the hotel where she planned to meet her lover.

Right there in that hotel, John Sutcliffe humiliated his wife in the presence of Peter and other onlookers who came out to witness the ruckus. The episode only went further to cement Peter's idea of what women were to him and men in general. His attitude towards women changed after knowing about his mother's infidelity to her husband.

Peter's First attempted murder

Peter started visiting brothels around Bradford to comfort himself after losing the adoration he once had for his mother. He became a frequent customer at the Red Light district of Yorkshire where he picked prostitutes and found solace in their arms throughout the night. But his tenderness with these women did not last long as he would soon discover the thrills associated with murdering them in cold blood.

The first recorded case

Peter's first attacked a woman sometime in 1969. He'd called one of his friends, Trevor Birdsaw, to complain about a sex worker that owed him money and was refusing to pay. The two of them got into Peter's car and drove through Leeds in search of the woman, until Peter suddenly stopped the car and jumped out. He asked Trevor to take over the wheels as he disappeared into the darkness to attack the lady who he had just sighted. Once he reached her, he whacked her on the back of the head and then ran back to the car drenched in sweat.

Few days later, police came to question Peter about his whereabouts on the day the sex worker was attacked. Peter never denied it. He claimed that he'd dealt the woman a slight blow on her head using his hands.

Fortunately, the sex worker survived her wounds, but she never came out to testify against Peter due to her line of work and not wanting any more trouble from the authorities. Peter walked free without any disciplinary actions. If he had been arrested and charged with assault against a woman, the police may have saved several other women from the terror that was about to come on them in the hands of this serial killer.

The Real Reign of Terror begins

There is no assurance that Peter took any life or attacked anybody between 1969 and 1975. He seemed to be quiet within those years, but those where definitely the years he spent polishing his modus operandi.

By October 1975, he was ready to put himself out there and commit his first murder. Peter lived with his wife during this period and he supported their small family through his job as a long-distance truck driver. This meant that he spent a lot of nights away from the house, and he would stop along various brothels to satisfy himself with the women there.

Wilma McCann

It was around this time that the body of 28-year-old Wilma McCann was found in a local park in Leeds, on the 30th of October 1975. Wilma had recently come in from Scotland to work as a sex worker in Yorkshire. Life was quite hard for her and her four children and she felt that the only way she could raise some money was by prostitution, so she continued on that path on until she met her unfortunate end in the hands of Peter Sutcliffe.

Peter's attack on Wilma informed a killing pattern that would be used by the killer for the rest of his spree. His method was to strike his victim with a ball pain hammer multiple times on the back of the head until they fell unconscious. Then he would stab them with his screwdriver. In Wilma's case, he stabbed her about 15 times on the neck, chest and abdomen. After days of investigation, Wilma's case went cold since the police couldn't find anything to help them identify the killer.

Emily Jackson

Three months later, on the 20th of January 1976, the Yorkshire Ripper struck again. His second victim was a woman murdered in Leeds. Emily Jackson was a 42-year-old wife and mother who disappeared after a night out at a local pub in Leeds. The killer employed almost the same killing method he had used on his first victim. He'd struck Emily multiple times before going ahead to stab her about 50 times all over her upper body with a screwdriver. At the time of her death, Emily was working at as a sex worker to support her family, just like Wilma. It is possible that Peter approached her as a client before deciding to take her life.

But in Emily's case, the police were able to discover a small piece of evidence they could hold on to with the hope of apprehending the killer. Right there on Emily's thighs, they found the prints from the sole of a 7 Wellington boot. During their struggle, the killer had, for some reason, stamped on her thigh with a great force that almost dislocated her joints. He never knew that he had left a visible imprint on her thighs.

The police got down to work and tried to trace the boot by contacting the manufacturers. The wanted to find out people who had bought the boots and the places it may have travelled to. Unfortunately, all their efforts remained futile and nothing came out of that investigation. Just like Wilma, Emily's case went cold again.

For a while after Emily, the Yorkshire Ripper seemed to calm down with his killing spree. But it didn't last too long. A year after Emily's death, Peter struck again, murdering his next victim with a similar modus operando.

Irene Richardson

Irene Richardson's body was discovered in Leeds on the 5th of February, 1977. The 28-year-old had been brutally murdered with a hammer and stabbed two times with a screwdriver. Just like the other victims, Irene had been a sex worker at the time of her death. With this third victim, the police came to a conclusion that they were dealing with a serial killer on the loose. They didn't realize that with Irene's murder, their villain was just warming up. Many more recorded cases would come into the picture sooner than later.

Patricia Atkinson

Less than three months after the murder of Irene Richardson, Peter dealt his next blow on the Bradford community. On the 23rd of April, 1977, 32-year-old Patricia Atkinson became his fourth victim. Her dead body was found in her own flat in Bradford, where the murder had taken place.

Patricia had stopped entertaining her customers outside of her home, believing that it was safer to have them in her flat, since the killer was known to kill prostitutes in dark alleys and deserted parks.

Sadly, her safety precautions did her no good. Her luck ran out when the man she invited into her flat turned out to be the killer she was avoiding. The killer hit her five times on her skull with his signature hammer, after which he savagely mutilated her body with a small pen knife.

When the police found her in her flat, they were also able to come across some tangible clues that could help them. They saw the exact same boot prints on the bedsheets in Patricia's room as the one they'd seen on Emily's thighs. This link was the final confirmation needed to draw a conclusion. The Yorkshire Ripper was expanding his territory and his killer instincts were running wide. He seemed to know the kind of women he wanted – sex workers, since his last four victims had been working as such before their death.

He found them to be vulnerable, easy preys that he could convince into his car before driving away with them. Once in his car, he would check around to ensure that no one was watching before going about his business of killing them off.

Jane McDonald

At least, the police thought so, too, until the body of a 16-year-old, Jane McDonald was found one morning by children in a playground.

When the news went live on the 26th of June 1977, the nation was in clear shock.

This murder happened barely two months after Patricia's, and this time the killer targeted a minor who wasn't a sex worker like his other victims. The general public's perception of the killer started to change after the attack on the school girl. It was obvious to them that their killer wasn't just a night killer looking to murder vulnerable women he found alone in dark alleys.

Jane's death caused a public outcry in Britain as a whole, and it was at this time the tabloid came up with the nickname 'The Yorkshire Ripper', reminiscent of Jack, The Ripper.

Jane's death sparked up conversations about safety on major TV stations. The press only became interested in reporting about the killings after her death. The nation had never seen anything of that sort since Jack, the Ripper and it seemed like something intriguing that could help the press make some quick money.

The real outrage came after some newspapers described Jane as the killer's first innocent victim, like the other women had done something to deserve the death they got. That report angered many women groups and other feminists who were out to protect women's right. It was obvious that the police only started to take the killing seriously after Jane's death, and that shouldn't have been the case.

Jane's death also increased the fear in the women of Leeds and Bradford where most of the murders had taken place. As the killings went on, the fear heightened to an extent where women became scared to leave their homes at night. Their fear led to them questioning their husbands and boyfriends, asking them about their whereabouts on the day a particular murder had taken place.

The attention from the media only succeeded in increasing the torture faced by the families of the deceased. Everywhere you went, there were posters with their names, asking the public to help capture the Yorkshire Ripper. There was absolutely no way their loved ones could get away from all the media scrutiny that came with their deaths.

By now, the desperation to catch the killer had increased. A full-scale manhunt had been created by the Yorkshire police department to capture the killer and prevent further deaths. But then, it seemed he was indeed a smart one.

Jean Jordan

On the morning of the 9th of October, 1977, the body of 20-year-old sex worker, Jean Jordan, was discovered on an allotment in Manchester. By the time her mutilated body was found, she had been dead for six days.

But this time, the detectives were in luck. They found a newly minted five-pound note in in Jean's handbag, and this clue led them to Bradford. After further investigation, the police found themselves in front of Peter Sutcliffe's house. They'd traced the note via the issuing bank and discovered that it had passed through the hands of over 300 people, one of them being Peter.

Peter was interviewed, but he claimed to be at a family party on the night Jean was murdered. His family members confirmed the story to the police. The detectives never knew that they already had their culprit in their grasp, but he was slipping away gradually. This would be the first of many times Peter would escape discovery from the police after numerous clues that led to him.

His first escape from the police may have emboldened him as Peter killed about three more women between December 1977 and June 1978, their skulls bludgeoned until their death. As usual, all his victims were sex workers. After this three extra murders, Peter may have felt invincible, almost undiscoverable by the police and this gave him the courage to continue in his killing spree.

The detectives are careless once again

The ripper picked up another victim on December 14th 1977, but this time she would narrowly escape death in his hands. Marilyn Moore described her attacker in full details to the police and his face was sketched out and released. Of course, the picture led the Yorkshire police to Peter about seven different times during their manhunt, yet, for an inexplicable reason, they continued to rule him out.

Detective George Oldfield's (the detective in charge of the Yorkshire Ripper's case) had become too distracted by the Wearside Jack, a British man with a Wearside accent who sent over an audio cassette in which he claimed to be the Ripper. The audio recording taunted the police and mocked George's effort to catch the killer.

His tape disrupted investigations and forced detectives to look away from Yorkshire and focus on the Northwest Wearside where the accent was most prominent. Because of the tape, the police let Peter Sutcliffe out of their list of suspects since he didn't have the accent. They didn't know that audio from Wearside Jack was only a hoax and it would give Peter enough time to kill more women.

The Ripper Strikes again

With the attention of the detectives now divided, the Yorkshire Ripper struck again. His newest victim was discovered in April 1979. Her body had been heavily mutilated with multiple stab wounds and cracks on her skull. Josephine Whitaker, a 19-year-old building society worker was his 10th victim.

In August that year, the West Yorkshire detectives once again visited Peter for questioning. The reason for their new questions was because Peter's car had been sighted in three red light areas in Leeds, Bradford and Manchester.

The detective noted how cold he was while talking to them, his answers always direct and with nothing more to them. He never volunteered more information than he was asked and it seemed he was hiding something from the police. They described him as a well-groomed man who had no charisma or welcoming personality around him. They also noticed that Peter had a gap in his teeth that made his dentition resemble that found on two of the victims.

Their encounter with Peter left them with a lot of suspicion. A report was submitted to senior officers that suggested Peter needed to be investigated further. The report was blatantly rejected by senior officers who were so convinced that the killer was the mysterious Wearside Jack. Other suspects were gingerly dismissed as distractions. This avoidable mistake would lead to the death of three more women.

The detectives spent most of their time trying to catch the Wearside Jack, when the killer they were looking for was just outside their backyard. They seemed confused for a minute. Unknown to them, they were following a wrong trail and chasing shadows. During this period, Peter escaped them about two more times, bringing his total number of escapes to nine.

Peter lied his way out of many interviews and questioning sessions. He was very good at cooking up stories and he always had an alibi to support his claim as to why he had been at certain places at certain times. Since he was a long distance driver, most of his excuses seemed plausible. He could be at odd places late at night and easily blame it on his line of work and it would make sense to any listener.

It seemed Peter himself was quite surprised with the fact that he hadn't been caught and the police still hadn't found a trail that led to him. During interviews after his apprehension, Peter said his multiple escapes gave him some kind of motivation to go on with the killings. It was like nature's stamp of approval on his atrocities. Something or someone was protecting him from ever getting caught. He may have believed he would walk a freeman for life even after all of his crimes.

Barbara Leach

As the police kept their focus on Wearside Jack, Peter started killing again. In September of 1979, the Yorkshire Ripper attacked a 20-year-old university student, Barbara Leach.

Barbara was murdered on the 2nd of September, 1979 after a night out with friends, just a few yards from the place she bid them goodbye and went on her way.

Barbara's death created a new wave of interest in the Ripper cases. The media coverage increased astronomically to such an extent that everywhere you went, there was always something to remind you of the Ripper. Large offers were made to anyone who could provide valuable information and help stop the killings.

During this period, the police had to compile all their collected information on log cards since they didn't have computers to help them out. And due to the popularity of the case, the police were inundated with incoming information from various sources, resulting in boxes and boxes of index cards which made sorting through quite difficult.

Marguerite Walls

While the police continued in their struggle to find credible information that could lead to an arrest, the Ripper seemed to have figured out his next move. After over a year of quietness, he struck again, on the 20th of August 1980 when the body of 47-year-old Marguerite Walls' was found in a dark alley at Leeds.

She had been struck on the back of her head, but the killer also employed another new killing method this time. The killer had used a rope to strangle her. Walls was found with marks around her neck that signified she'd struggled intensely before her death. Peter may have wanted to mislead the police and get them thinking that they were now dealing with a different kind of killer.

Marguerite Walls ended up as Peter's 12th victim, yet he walked free and the police still hadn't identified him.

Mo Lea's lucky escape and survival

In September 1980, Mo Lea moved from Liverpool to Leeds to complete her art degree. On arriving Leeds, friends told her stories about the killer of Yorkshire and warned her about being alone at odd hours of the day and in isolated places. Mo herself noticed the dead air that hung around Leeds, and the fear that inhabited the people, especially women. The streets of Leeds became quieter after 8pm because no one could tell where the killer was and who he was targeting next.

The students of Leeds University made it a point of duty to protect each other by walking home together at night or sleeping over at each other's rooms if it became too late to walk on the streets.

A few days to her birthday, October 25th 1980, Mo and her friends met in a pub somewhere in Chapel town area of Leeds to discuss and make plans to celebrate her birthday.

Around 10 pm, the group ended their conversation and left the pub. Mo's friends volunteered to walk her into the safer part of the town where she would get a bus, but she assured them that she would be alright.

Along the way, Mo decided to take a shortcut that would get her to town faster. What she didn't know was that there was a dark figure lurking in the shadows, a screwdriver in his hand.

Halfway through her journey, Mo heard a friendly male voice call out from behind, asking how she was doing. She stopped and turned to face him, but his figure didn't strike her as familiar. The way he kept talking made Mo think he was someone she knew, so she stood and waited as he approached her. By the time she realized he was a stranger, he had come too close to her.

Mo turned and started to walk away from him as quickly as possible, but then she heard his footsteps hasten just behind her. The faster she tried to move, the closer the man got to her until she felt a heavy whack on her head that knocked her unconscious.

Luck being on her side, some students were approaching the same road just as she was being attacked and they heard her scream. Peter took off once he saw them coming.

The next time Mo realized herself, she was lying on a hospital bed. Even her parents were unable to recognize her due to the terrible injuries that masked her face. She had a broken jaw with a slight crack on her skull and some bruises all over her face.

Jacqueline Hills

While the police tried to contemplate and link Mo Lea's attack to the ripper, another victim in Leeds lost her life on the 17th of November 1980. 20-year-old Jacqueline Hill would end up as Peter Sutcliffe's last victim. She was found dead with multiple stab wounds on her neck and her body had been horribly mutilated. Her wounds bore a strong resemblance to those found on the other victims of the Ripper.

The Yorkshire Ripper is caught

The ripper's luck soon ran out on the day he intended to kill another woman, just two months after attacking Mo Lea.

His sensational arrest happened just at the dawn of the 1981 new year. Peter had gone over to Sheffield where he picked up a sex worker. The two of them got into a car and drove off to an unknown destination. Around that same time, a policeman and a new recruit were driving along the road and chatting about the new job. One of them spotted Peter's car close to their office at Melbourne Avenue in Sheffield red light district and decided to stop him for a chat.

When they reached the two occupants of the car, the policemen greeted and asked who they were. Peter spoke and claimed that he had just only met the lady he had in his car. The situation seemed strange and odd and the policeman asked the pair to get down from the car for a search.

Peter said he needed to urinate while they search the lady in his car. The policemen showed him a side of the road where he could ease himself.

While Peter was away, the officer did a PNC check on his registration number and discovered that the plates were false. Peter was arrested immediately and taken to Dewsbury Police station.

He was search at the station and they found nothing incrementing on him, but the officers decided not to let him go away so easily. They recognized Peter from the different times they'd gone over to question him at his home in Bradford.

Two detectives were sent over to the spot where he'd been arrested to check if he dropped any weapon when he said he needed to urinate. The found his hammer and a screwdriver at the site and brought them back to the station.

At this point, Peter knew it was over. His long game was coming to an end, gradually crashing down on him. He eventually gave up and agreed to confess to his murders, but only on one condition: That the police would call his wife, Sonya, and tell her about his atrocities before she heard them on the news.

Before the new morning, many major news outlets had gotten hold of the information and it started circulating around Yorkshire and Britain as a whole. Peter's arrest brought an end to the almost five years of killings since his first victim's life was taken in 1976.

The police now had the Yorkshire Ripper in their hands and the women of Leeds and Bradford could breathe a sigh of relief.

The arrest came with a lot of jubilation, but no one could have been happier than Officer Andrew Laptew who had suggested that further investigations be carried out on Sutcliffe after his interview at his home. He had been right all the while, but the senior officers never paid him any attention. The case could have been closed a long time ago.

The Yorkshire Murders was the biggest mystery murder case in Britain since the Moors Murders, and the press was having a swell time with it. Peter Sutcliffe's face was everywhere, making headlines on top new stations in Britain and other parts of Europe.

Mo Lea was at home watching the news when the story about the Yorkshire Ripper came on. They caught his face from a camera shot while he was being led into a Prison Van and she began to cry instantly. She recognized Peter Sutcliffe as the man who attacked her on the 25th of October, 1980.

Peter Sutcliffe's Trial

After his arrest, Peter Sutcliffe was remanded at the Gooseberry Magistrate Court, on January 5th, 1981 for the murder of Jacqueline Hill. Few weeks later, he was charged with 13 murders and another six attempted murders.

To save himself from spending a lifetime in prison, Peter began to claim insanity. He told all who listened that a voice from above had commanded him to clear the streets of prostitutes. Peter wished to be sent to the comfort of a secure hospital where he would have a better life than a prison where he could get killed by other inmates.

At his preliminary hearing on the 29th of April, 1981, at the Central Criminal Court of England and Wales in London, Peter pleaded not guilty to murder but guilty to manslaughter on the grounds of diminished responsibility.

The trial Judge listened to evidence from psychiatrists from the prosecution and defense end before asking members of the jury to apply caution while dealing with Peter's case and to be very careful when taking words from a serial killer.

At the end, Peter Sutcliffe was made to stand trial on the charges of murder and attempted murder.

Peter's trial before a jury began on the 5th of May, 1981. Before he arrived the court in a police van, crowds were already seated outside waiting for him for hours. Some reporters had spent the night right there in front of the court in anticipation for the drama of the next day.

The trial lasted 14 days and the jury reached a decision that Peter Sutcliffe was guilty of all charges levied against him.

Throughout the court hearing, it remained obvious to everyone on ground that Peter Sutcliffe was quite aware of everything he was doing as he killed those women. After killing and getting away with it, he would return to commit another murder within mere months. And he always arrived a crime scene fully prepared, with his signature weapons.

On the 22nd of May 1981, Peter Sutcliffe was given 20 life sentences and a minimum of 30 years' imprisonment before any consideration for parole. He was shipped off to the Isle of Wright to start his prison sentence at the Parkhurst prison.

Battle with mental health and death

In 1984, Peter was diagnosed with paranoid schizophrenia. It is widely speculated that he developed the symptoms in prison because of the stress he faced, being one of the most popular inmates in Parkhurst. He had survived a number of attacks from other inmates which led him to be on alert 24/7, with the belief that someone else was out to kill him. he lost his eye during one of such attacks in 1997. He was transferred to a hospital in Berkshire for treatment.

On October 29, 2020, Peter Sutcliffe was rushed from the Frankland Jail to the University Hospital of North Durham after suffering a heart attack. Later, he tested positive to COVID 19 and refused to receive treatment for the sickness. Two weeks later, on the 13th of November, 2020, Peter Sutcliffe died in the hospital after his lungs collapsed.

Till the day of his death, Sutcliffe never gave any reason for attacking and killing any of those women. In fact, he continued to deny his attack on Mo Lea until his death. But one thing is sure, this man commonly referred to as the Yorkshire Ripper ruined many lives during his time here on earth and he will go down as one of the most dangerous men to ever walk the streets of West Yorkshire.

References

Bolton, M. (2012). *Wicked Beyond Belief: The Hunt for the Yorkshire Ripper*. HarperCollins.

Carter, C., & Hyde, N. (2020, November 13). *How Peter Sutcliffe became Yorkshire's most notorious murderer and the victims we must always remember*. Retrieved from Leedslive.

Cobb, R. C. (2019). *On the trail of the Yorkshire Ripper*. Philadelphia: Pen and Sword True Crime.

Engelbrecht, G. (2020, November 13). *The Northern Echo*. Retrieved from In profile: The twisted life of the Yorkshire Ripper Peter Sutcliffe.

Famousbio. (n.d.). *Peter Sutcliffe - Criminals, Life Achievements and Facts*. Retrieved from famousbio.

In profile: Yorkshire Ripper Peter Sutcliffe's twisted life following his death aged 74. (2020, November 13). Retrieved from Independent.

Kavanagh, J. (2021, March 4). *Twister Killer: Who was the Yorkshire Ripper and what was Peter Sutcliffe's cause of death*. Retrieved from The Sun.

Kirka, D. (2020, November 13). *UK's Yorkshire Ripper Serial Killer Peter Sutcliffe dies*. Retrieved from Daily Mountain Eagle.

Mudie, K., & Kitching, C. (2020, November 13). *Yorkshire Ripper Dead: Serial Killer Peter Sutcliffe dies after battle with Covid - 19* . Retrieved from The Mirror .

Nguyen, S. (2020 , December 16). *Who was the Yorkshire Ripper? What to know before watching the Ripper on Nteflix* . Retrieved from Yahoo!life .

Let us hear your thoughts

If you enjoyed this book, please support Gerald Burns by going over to Amazon to drop a short and honest review. It would be fully appreciated. Also help us in spreading the word in any way possible by getting more people to read this book. It would mean the world to us.

Thank you very much!

Other Books by Gerald Burns

Enter the killer psychology of Britain's most famous and prolific serial killer who was killing at least one person per week at the height of his murder spree.

On June 24 1998 Angela Woodruff received news of her mother's death from the family doctor. He stated that her mother's lifeless body had been found lying peacefully in her home where she lived alone. The family doctor advised Angela that no autopsy would be required and that it would be better if her mother's corpse was cremated. Angela refused, asking instead that her mother's body be buried.

Mrs. Woodruff was a solicitor at Hyde and she was remained in charge of her mother's affairs for a larger part of her life, so it came as quite the shock when she discovered that another will existed and this one stated that all of her mother's estate be handed over to the family's doctor. Angela now knew that her mother had been murdered and a will forged to claim benefits from her death. All findings pointed to Dr. Harold Fredrick Shipman. This would be his last murder out of over 218 others.

Dr. Harold Fredrick Shipman's patients likened the news of making it to his patient's list to winning the UK lottery. He was kind, caring and always ready to visit and listen to his elderly patients. What they didn't know was that this kind-looking doctor was picking them off his list as he kindly took their lives.

HYDE'S KILLER DOCTOR navigates the life and times of Britain's most prolific and charming serial killer. Gerald Burns' narrative power comes alive as he takes you through the mind of this killer doctor who killed his victims with all the kindness he could muster.

About The Author

Gerald Burns' obsession with true crime stories and the dark psychology of serial killers started on a flight to flight to New York in 2004 while reading a book on the Manson murders. Few months later he read a story about a young waitress who had gone missing after her shift, never to be seen again. She simply vanished.

Since then he became interested in true crimes stories, stories of disappearances and the weird histories of the world. He started writing out about some of these disappearances in magazines and had people send in their suggestions and thoughts about the cases. The interest for this led him to start writing out some of these stories for the enjoyment of other true crime addicts.

You can connect with him on Twitter, Instagram and Facebook.

Printed in Great Britain
by Amazon